I Want to Be a
TYRANNOSAURUS REX

by Thomas Kingsley Troupe

illustrated by Jomike Tejido

PICTURE WINDOW BOOKS
a capstone imprint

My stomach rumbled in the lunch line at school. I was hungry for pizza, but they weren't serving it today.

"We just had pizza yesterday, Tyrone," my friend Riley said. "They can't make that all the time."

"Yeah, I guess," I said. I got a sandwich and a fruit cup, but I wasn't happy.

I bit into the sandwich. It had mayonnaise on it. Yuck! "I want to be a Tyrannosaurus rex," I shouted. "Then I can eat whatever I want!"

3

In an instant, I became a Tyrannosaurus rex! How did that even happen? I kicked over a lunch table by accident. Kids from my school ran, scared of me.

It was like a monster was loose in the school—and the monster was me! I had to escape before I hurt someone.

The world around me changed. I was in a river valley. Little lizard creatures ran away from me. A herd of Triceratops looked at me with nervous eyes.

Whoa! Was I in the prehistoric past? Where was I supposed to find pizza in the time of the dinosaurs?

WAAAAY BACK . . . WHEN? Tyrannosaurus rex stomped around Earth during the late Cretaceous Period. This period started 145.5 to 65.5 million years ago. Other well-known dinosaurs that lived during this time included Triceratops, Stegoceras, Spinosaurus, and Velociraptor.

5

I needed to get back home. When I turned and took a step, the ground trembled under my feet. My head felt as big as a wrecking ball.

In the distance I heard big footsteps. Another T. rex stomped my way!

"Oh, great," the T. rex said. "Another big mouth to eat everything! Perfect."

"Hi," I said and waved my tiny arms. "I'm Tyrone."

"Yeah? Well, I'm Hank," he said. When Hank turned, he almost hit me with his tail!

The older T. rex didn't seem very friendly. But since I didn't know any others like me, I hung around.

"You're not following me, are you?" Hank asked. "I can't have you getting in the way of my meals, kid."

I thought about pizza again. I waved my little arms. They were super tiny compared to my giant body. "How am I supposed to pick up food with these?"

Hank groaned. "You're not going to make fun of the arms, are you? The other dinosaurs like to joke around about them."

"Really?"

"Yeah, but trust me, kid," Hank said. "Forget about those little arms. When it comes to eating, our big mouths take care of business."

Hank was right. I could feel about 60 teeth in there! They weren't sharp, but they felt banana-shaped.

LIFT SOME WEIGHTS, T! Scientists aren't sure what purpose the T. rex's little arms served. Its bite, however, was the strongest of any land animal that ever lived!

"I'm getting kind of hungry," I said. I never finished my sandwich at school.

"Of course you are," Hank said. He was stomping toward some bushes, sniffing the air. "And there's something tasty, now!"

I saw a few baby Triceratops playing on their own. Hank went after them, but I tripped him with my tail.

"Hey," I shouted. "You can't eat babies! That's not even fair."

Hank wasn't happy. "We eat whatever we want," he said. He sniffed and found a bigger, dead dinosaur on the ground.

"Looks like leftovers again," Hank said and began to eat. I couldn't watch!

"Gross," I whispered.

"What are you waiting for, kid? Dig in!" Hank said. I wasn't hungry anymore!

13

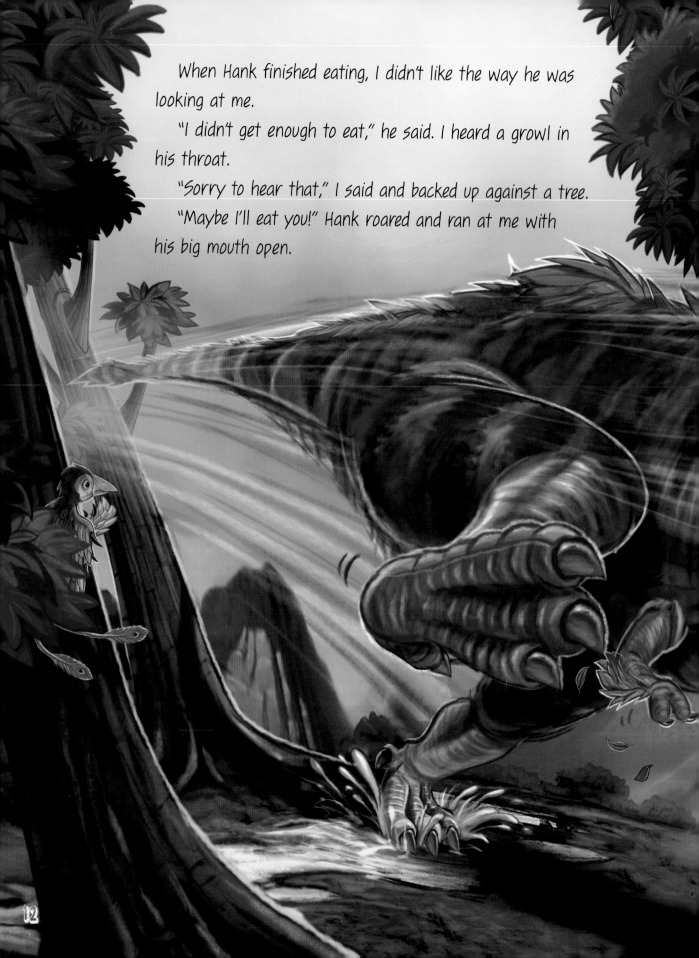

When Hank finished eating, I didn't like the way he was looking at me.

"I didn't get enough to eat," he said. I heard a growl in his throat.

"Sorry to hear that," I said and backed up against a tree.

"Maybe I'll eat you!" Hank roared and ran at me with his big mouth open.

I dodged his toothy attack. Hank missed me and sank his teeth into a giant tree.

"Ugh!" Hank roared. Splinters flew from his jaws as he shook his head. "I hate plants!"

I ran for the river. With friends like Hank, I wouldn't last long in prehistoric times.

NOT SO FAST! Though it had giant legs, many scientists think T. rex could only run about 10 miles (16 kilometers) per hour.

Far from Hank, I found a mama Tyrannosaurus rex and a few of her babies. The mom stepped toward me. She looked angry too.

Were there any friendly T. rexes?

"Don't even think about eating my babies," Mama T said.

"I won't," I promised. "I'm hungry for pizza."

The little ones looked strange and . . . furry. There were downy feathers all over their bodies. There was also a large mound of leaves and torn up vines.

Mama T watched her little ones and the mound carefully. An egg was nestled under all of those rotten plants!

"What's with the stinky leaves?" I asked.

"Rotting vegetation helps keep the eggs warm," Mama T explained.

HOW DO YOU LIKE YOUR EGGS? Some scientists think that T. rex mothers covered their eggs in rotting vegetation to help keep them toasty warm, just like some birds do today.

I found another T. rex wandering around. He seemed older, but was much friendlier than Hank. His legs looked thin, and his head hung kind of low.

"I'm always hungry," he said. "I've been looking for meals for almost 30 years. Now I'm getting too old to hunt and fight."

He and I kept walking, watching the other dinosaurs eat plants and strange fruits. I was really hungry now, but none of those plants looked good to me. I'd thought a T. rex could eat whatever it wanted. But what if it didn't like what was on the menu?

I looked around at the trees and swamps. I really wanted to get home and order a pizza for dinner. I wondered where Saucy's Pizza Place would be millions of years from now. Was I in a prehistoric version of my own neighborhood?

BONE-NANZA! Tyrannosaurs rex roared and stomped around North America. More than 50 skeletons of the mighty T. rex have been found in Colorado, South Dakota, Montana, and Utah.

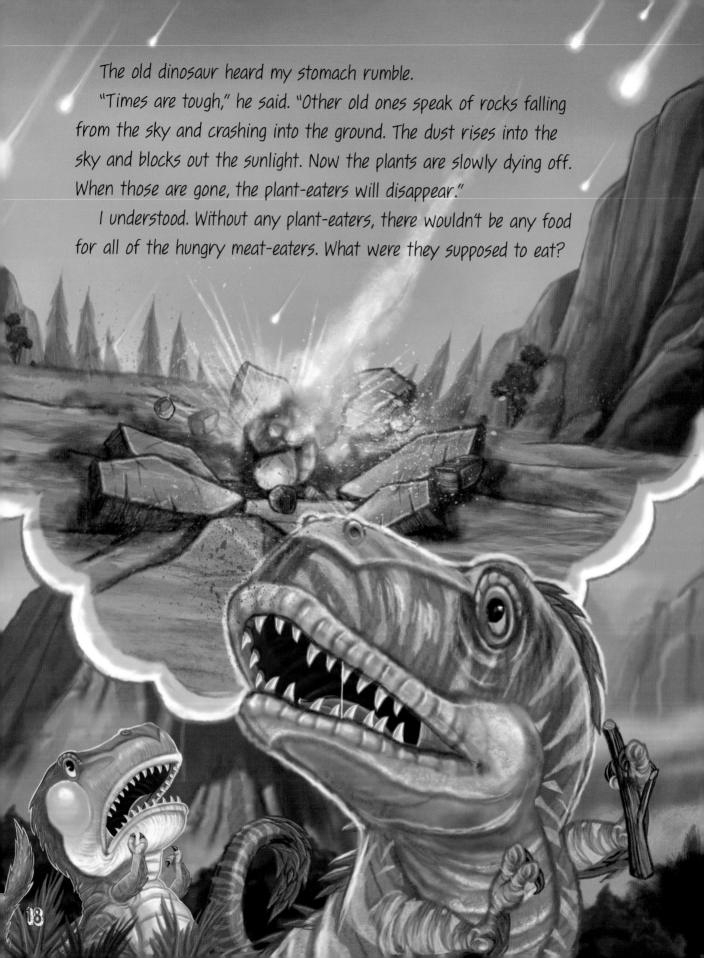

The old dinosaur heard my stomach rumble.

"Times are tough," he said. "Other old ones speak of rocks falling from the sky and crashing into the ground. The dust rises into the sky and blocks out the sunlight. Now the plants are slowly dying off. When those are gone, the plant-eaters will disappear."

I understood. Without any plant-eaters, there wouldn't be any food for all of the hungry meat-eaters. What were they supposed to eat?

As I thought about food, I blinked. And just like that, I was back at school. Riley looked at me funny.

"Hey, Ty," he said. "Are you going to eat your lunch or what?"

"Oh, yeah," I said and took a giant, dinosaur-sized bite of my sandwich. After being a T. rex, school lunch never tasted so good!

GOING EXTINCT STINKS! Some scientists think meteorite strikes and erupting volcanoes may have led to dinosaurs dying out. Large amounts of ash and dust from these events would have blocked out sunlight. Without sunlight, plants—and the dinosaurs that ate them—would have died out.

MORE ABOUT TYRANNOSAURUS REX

The word Tyrannosaurus means "tyrant lizard."

The most complete T. rex skeleton ever found was nicknamed "Sue" after paleontologist Sue Hendrickson. It was 13 feet (4 meters) tall and 40 feet (12.19 meters) long. Scientists think Sue weighed as much as 9 tons (8.2 metric tons)!

Tyrannosaurus rex was at the top of the food chain. It didn't have predators to worry about. Old age, disease, and hunger were its worst enemies.

T. rex rarely stood up straight. It walked horizontally, using its tail to balance its heavy head.

Tyrannosaurus rex could eat up to 500 pounds (227 kilograms) of meat in one bite. Its teeth crushed bones as it bit into its prey. Scientists know this because broken bones have been found in its dung!

Scientists have found very few baby dinosaur skeletons. This fact leads them to think that large meat-eating dinosaurs, such as T. rex, liked to eat babies!

Tyrannosaurus rex had a rotten mouth! Some scientists think that the bacteria-infected meat stuck in their teeth made their bites poisonous, just like the bite from a Komodo dragon today. Some dinosaurs likely survived a bite only to die of infection later.

GLOSSARY

bacteria—very small living things that exist all around you and inside you; some bacteria cause disease

downy—covered with fine, soft hair or feathers

dung—solid waste from animals

extinct—no longer living; an extinct animal is one that has died out, with no more of its kind

herd—a large group of animals that lives or moves together

horizontal—flat and parallel to the ground

infection—an illness caused by germs such as bacteria or viruses

meteorite—a piece of meteor that falls all the way to the ground

paleontologist—a scientist who studies fossils

predator—an animal that hunts other animals for food

prehistoric—from a time before history was recorded

tyrant—someone who rules other people in a cruel or unjust way

vegetation—plant life

READ MORE

Sabatino, Michael. *T. rex vs. Crocodile.* Bizarre Beast Battles. New York: Gareth Stevens Publishing, 2016.

Stewart, Melissa. *Why Did T. rex Have Short Arms?: And Other Questions about ... Dinosaurs.* Good Question! New York: Sterling Children's Books, 2014.

Wegwerth, A. L. *Tyrannosaurus rex.* Little Paleontologist. North Mankato, Minn.: Capstone Press, 2015.

INTERNET SITES

FactHound offers a safe, fun way to find internet sites related to this book. All of the sites on FactHound have been researched by our staff.

Here's all you do:
Visit *www.facthound.com*
Type in this code: 9781479587674

Check out projects, games and lots more at
www.capstonekids.com

INDEX

BOOKS IN THE SERIES

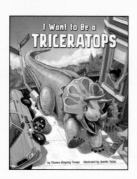

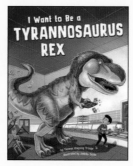

Dedication
To Jake, who is known to sometimes eat like a T. rex!

Thanks to our adviser for his expertise, research, and advice:
Mathew J. Wedel, PhD
Associate Professor
Western University of Health Services

Editors: Christopher Harbo and Anna Butzer
Designer: Sarah Bennett
Art Director: Ashlee Suker
Production Specialist: Kathy McColley

The illustrations in this book were planned with pencil on paper and finished with digital paints.

Picture Window Books are published by Capstone,
1710 Roe Crest Drive, North Mankato, Minnesota 56003
www.capstonepub.com

Library of Congress Cataloging-in-Publication Data
Catalogue-in-publication information is on file with the Library of Congress.

ISBN 978-1-4795-8767-4 (library binding)
ISBN 978-1-4795-8771-1 (eBook PDF)

Summary: Follows a young boy as he transforms into a Tyrannosaurus rex and experiences life from a dinosaur's perspective.

Printed and bound in the USA.
009685F16